Johann

Swiss Family Robinson

Adapted by H.Q. Mitchell

mm publications

Introduction

Johann David Wyss was a priest in Berne, Switzerland. He was born on 28 May 1743, he spoke four languages and had four sons; he loved nature and often took the boys on long walks and hunting trips. He also enjoyed reading to his children and wrote stories for their entertainment.

Swiss Family Robinson was created for his sons who loved adventures like Daniel Defoe's *The Life and Adventures of Robinson Crusoe* (1719).

Johann David Wyss based the characters in the story on his own family, so the main characters are a pastor with his wife and four sons. The writer wanted to teach his sons about the importance of respecting nature and seeking knowledge as well as about human kindness, so, he uses the story to talk about these things and teach a lesson to his children.

However, the story remained incomplete and disorganised, as it was created mainly for entertainment.

When he grew older, Johann Rudolf Wyss found his father's manuscript of the story and got his permission to edit and publish it. Another son, Johann Emmanuel Wyss, made illustrations and the book was finally published in German in 1812. It became popular and was translated into English in 1814. Along with the various translations, came numerous adaptations of the book, which offer variations and different endings of the story.

There have been various adaptations of the story in books, TV series and films. The basic ideas however, are these of survival, family love and love for nature.

Contents

CHAPTER 1

Lieutenant Bell has been a sailor for many years. He's spent a long time at sea and he's faced a lot of difficulties on his voyages; pirates are a great danger, and there have been terrifying moments during storms, when huge waves nearly swallowed his ship, the Adventurer.

"If you love me and our children, you won't go on another voyage," his wife keeps begging, urging him to stop travelling and find a job on land.

"If you love me, then you know that what you ask is impossible," he always answers. "The sea is my life and I cannot imagine myself away from it."

During his last trip, Lieutenant Bell kept remembering his wife's words as the Adventurer struggled with waves the size of mountains. The ship was travelling in the South Seas when a terrible storm started, blowing it far away and off its course. For three days the ship shook, tossed here and there by wild winds and everybody thought they were lost forever.

Then, suddenly a voice was heard. "Land ahead!" A strip of land was visible far away, and the crew managed to take the ship there and anchor it. It was a quiet, natural port on what looked like an island.

"We can stay here for a while and repair our ship," said Captain Johnson. "When the storm stops, we'll set sail again."

A little later, the men set off to explore. They were surprised to find a small boat and a tent house further up the shore. Inside were some clay pots and oyster shells, and also furniture and other comforts. It was clear that they were not the first men on the island.

"Lieutenant Bell!" called one of the men, as he came out of a small forest nearby. He rushed towards the officer, followed by a middle-aged stranger dressed in European clothes and carrying a big leather bag. The stranger looked friendly, even though he had a gun.

"Finally, after all these years!" cried the man in a trembling voice. "Thank God you are here!"

"My goodness," the lieutenant thought. "It's Robinson Crusoe himself!"

The man was a Swiss pastor who had been shipwrecked with his wife and four children when their ship crashed onto a rock. The crew had disappeared in the storm and they were nowhere to be seen afterwards.

"We were extremely lucky to be saved together as a family," said the pastor. "We were on our way to Australia to start a new life but, instead of that, we had to start a new life on this island. We have been here for four years," he added.

Lieutenant Bell told him that the ship was on its way to England when the storm stopped them.

"Would you like to come aboard?" asked Bell. "You can meet the captain and discuss your family's rescue with him," he suggested.

"We can all meet here tomorrow morning," answered the man. "I should return to my family and prepare them for our departure," he explained. "I did not want to alarm them when I saw your ship through my looking glass, so they don't know anything about it yet. I must hurry home and tell them. The boys will be thrilled!" he said with a big smile.

Then he took a diary out of his bag and put it in Lieutenant Bell's hands.

"Here is our story," he said. "If something happens, I would like you to give this to my brother in Switzerland. Now I must go," he added. "There is so much to do!"

7

CHAPTER 2

THE STORM THAT THE PASTOR'S FAMILY HAD BEEN CAUGHT IN was similar to the one that had brought the Adventurer to the island. For seven days their ship fought with monstrous waves but the strong winds blew it further and further off its course.

The ship shook and tossed out of control until it finally crashed onto a rock. Nothing could be done to move it from where it was stuck. The crew feared that they would sink. "Save yourselves!" cried the captain. "Quick! Get on the lifeboats!"

The boats were filling up quickly, so the pastor rushed to get his family. "Be brave, dear ones," he yelled as he led them to the deck.

Unfortunately, when the family went up on deck to board the lifeboats, the ship's crew had already disappeared. They realised that they were alone.

"Have they forgotten us?" cried Franz, the youngest of the boys, who was six years old. "What will happen to us now?"

The father advised his family to stay calm. Exhausted and afraid, the boys finally fell asleep. The pastor and Elizabeth, his wife, stayed awake, thinking of ways to save the family.

The first rays of morning light brought fresh hope. The family were thankful that the wind had stopped and they were relieved to see some land nearby. "It looks like an island," said the pastor.

"Let's swim to land while the sea is calm," suggested the fourteen-year old Fritz.

"That may be easy for you," said the second son, 12-year-old Ernest. "You are a strong swimmer, but the rest of us aren't. Why not build a raft?"

"Great idea, Ernest," said the pastor. "Now, let's all search through the ship for equipment to build a small raft. You should also look for anything that could be useful to take to the island," he added.

Fritz found guns and bullets. Ernest found nails, an axe, scissors, a hammer, and other building tools. Even young Franz found fishing hooks. Elizabeth announced that she had found and fed a cow, a donkey, six sheep and two goats. There were also some chickens, a rooster, geese and pigeons.

Suddenly, the third son, 10-year-old Jack was heard screaming. "Help! Help!" Two large dogs, Turk and Ponto, had leaped out of the captain's cabin. The pastor rushed to Jack only to find the two dogs jumping around happily. Jack laughed and rode on Turk's back "Hey, Daddy, it's like riding a horse!" he said. "The dogs will be useful for hunting once we get to the island, don't you think?" he said to his father.

"Yes, but first we need to get there," said the pastor.

"It doesn't look difficult," said Jack. "Put us all in a big tub and let us float to shore."

"A very good idea, Jack!" said the pastor. He remembered seeing eight empty casks on one of the ship's decks and now Jack's suggestion made him think of joining the casks together in order to create a boat made of barrels.

When he told his family about it, however, not everyone liked this idea. "I will never get into one of those!" cried Elizabeth.

However, she changed her mind as soon as she saw the whole thing finished. Once connected by two long pieces of wood, the raft finally floated. Each container held a family member while two other barrels carried gunpowder, a sail cloth and some chickens. The pigeons and geese were set free so they could fly to land, whereas the other animals had to be left behind.

"We'll feed them well now, and come back to get them in a few days' time," said the pastor.

Just as they were about to leave, the mother dropped a large mysterious bag into Franz's barrel.

"What's this?" asked the boy.

"Shh! It's my magic bag," whispered Elizabeth as she got into her barrel.

They waved goodbye to the animals and then something unexpected happened: Turk and Ponto jumped into the sea and swam all the way to the shore!

CHAPTER 3

THE FAMILY WAS NOW SAFELY ASHORE AND THEY ALL FELT relieved to be on land after so many weeks at sea. Once they found a river with fresh water nearby, they decided that this would be the most convenient place to pitch a tent. "Let's do this quickly, before it gets dark," said the pastor.

They used sail cloth from the ship for the tent and fishing hooks to fasten the entrance. "Our first home on this new land," said Elizabeth, as the boys collected dried grass to make beds with.

Closer to the river, they created a rough kitchen. The pastor made a fire using matches he had brought from the ship so that Elizabeth could boil some soup.

"What's that? It looks like soap or glue," noticed young Franz, pointing to some bars his mother was taking out of her bag.

"This looks like glue, but it is excellent meat," explained Elizabeth. "It has been cooked and turned to jelly. It is made this way so that it can be easily carried on long voyages. It is delicious, once we use it in our soup."

Jack went to the sea to look for shellfish that could also be served for dinner. It was not long before they heard a scream coming from the sea. The pastor rushed to see what was happening, only to find Jack up to his knees in the water with a lobster clasping his leg. "So you have found us food, Jack!" laughed the pastor.

The boy forgot his pain. "Can I take the lobster to mother?" he asked, smiling proudly. He managed to hold it, but suddenly, the lobster hit him with its tail. Jack got so angry that he picked up a stone and killed it.

"Why did you kill the animal with such hate?" asked the pastor.

"But it bit me!" said Jack.

"Don't you know that it was only trying to protect itself?" asked the pastor. The boy promised to be kinder and to control his anger in the future.

Then, he proudly gave the lobster to Elizabeth. "This will make dinner more delicious," he said.

"I've made soup, so we already have a good dinner," she said.

"Let's save the lobster for breakfast."

"I saw some oysters but don't want to get my feet wet," said Ernest.

"Well son, you will have to," said the pastor. "We must all work together even if this means wet feet or dirty hands."

A little later, Ernest came back with oysters, as well as salt he found on a rock. "Look at this!" he said. "Salt!" Unfortunately, the salt was mixed with dirt; however, Elizabeth added fresh water and then poured the liquid through a cloth to separate the salt from the dirt.

"Why don't we just use sea water rather than go to all this trouble?" asked Jack.

"Sea water is bitter and would spoil our dinner," explained the pastor.

As the family waited for Fritz to return from hunting, they wondered what they would use for spoons.

"I wish we had some coconuts," said Ernest. "We could use them as bowls."

"Wishing won't get you anywhere," said the pastor. "Have you got any other ideas?"

"We could use oyster shells for spoons," suggested Ernest. Everyone agreed that this was a very good idea, so Ernest set off to collect more oyster shells, saving the best one for himself.

Jack tried to open the shells by banging them on the ground, but with no success. His father showed him how to make them open by putting them near the fire. "The heat will make the oysters open," he said. Jack ate his first oyster. "Yuck. It tastes horrible," he said in disgust.

Later, Fritz returned from hunting with a small animal.

"I remember reading about this animal," said Ernest. "It's an agouti!"

"Yes, it's an agouti," The pastor agreed. "It is a fast animal that lives under the ground and eats fruit and nuts."

"Is it tasty?" asked Jack, who was always hungry.

"No, I'm afraid not. Its meat is hard and doesn't taste very nice," said the pastor.

After dinner, they heard the dogs snarling. They were attacking

14

the agouti. The family rushed to save it but it was too late. Fritz was so angry that he started screaming at the dogs and kicking them.

"Why are you behaving like this?" yelled the pastor to the boy. "The dogs are just hungry and do not know any better."

The boy stopped immediately and hung his head in shame. "But, Father, it's so unfair," he protested.

"That's nature's way, my son," said the pastor in a quiet voice. "I guess you'll find that out in time."

15

CHAPTER 4

AFTER A GOOD NIGHT'S SLEEP, THE PASTOR DECIDED THAT the day should be spent looking for the missing crew and exploring the area. The boys were excited to hear this. "Let's all go!" they begged.

"No," said the pastor. "Who knows what dangers there may be out there? Fritz and I will be able to travel much faster if we are alone. Don't worry about us. We'll be safe with our guns and Turk to protect us."

Fritz said that they should save the animals on the ship first. "A new storm could destroy the ship," he said. "The animals are better

than the people; they did not even think of us when they escaped from the ship!"

"Oh, Fritz!" said the pastor. "Just because the crew left, this does not mean that we should act cruelly. They may be in danger and need our help. Our animals, on the other hand, have food for a few more days and the ship doesn't seem to be in danger at the moment."

Fritz had to agree and then he got ready for the journey. They had not walked very far when Fritz exclaimed: "Coconuts! We will need to climb up, like those monkeys, in order to get some."

"That will take too long," said the pastor. "How about using the monkeys to do that for us?" He said and threw a few rocks at the monkeys. The little animals soon began throwing the fruit back at them. "Watch out! It's raining coconuts!" the pastor laughed as they ran behind a rock.

When the battle with the monkeys was over, the pastor and Fritz picked up the fresh coconuts from the ground. Fritz quickly opened one to taste some coconut milk, only to find that it was not as he expected. "Ernest will be disappointed," he said. "He thinks that coconut milk is a tasty drink. It probably will be, if you mix it with sugar; oh, if only I had some!"

His wish soon came true when a little later they found sugar cane. Mixed with sugar from the sugar cane, the coconut milk was really delicious. They poured some into their bottles to have for lunch and by midday found that the mixture in their bottles had become even sweeter. "The heat has made it tastier," explained the pastor. "Later, though, it will become sour because of fermentation." He was right. By night time, the delicious drink tasted like vinegar.

As they were exploring the forest, the pastor and Fritz also saw some gourds hanging from some tree trunks. "This fruit is very useful; its shell can be used to make bowls and even be joined together to make bottles," said the pastor. Right away, the father and son decided to use the gourds to make plates and kitchen utensils. Then, they filled them with sand and left them in the sun to dry.

"How do you know how to make these?" asked Fritz.

"I have seen plates like these at the Museum of London," said the pastor. "American Native people have been making these for centuries. I remember reading a book about this art."

"Well, Mother will surely appreciate it," said Fritz and smiled.

Their journey was coming to an end, and still they had found nothing. However, now that they had explored the place, the pastor and his son knew for certain that they were on an island. "I don't think people have ever been here before," said the pastor.

"How can you tell?" asked Fritz.

The pastor pointed to some pink flamingos standing calmly nearby. "The animals here don't seem frightened at all. They don't run away from us. You know, Fritz, animals are not naturally afraid of humans. They run away only after realising how dangerous people are," he said.

"Then, Father, we should try not to make the animals on the island afraid. We should only kill the ones that we must eat," said Fritz.

At that point, they heard Turk's snarls. They rushed to see what

was happening, and found the dog over a dead monkey. In the grass nearby, a baby monkey was watching in fear.

As soon as it saw them, the baby monkey jumped into Fritz's arms. The boy was moved by the orphan and hugged it, trying to make it feel better.

"Turk should be punished for killing this little monkey's mother," said Fritz.

"He did it because he needed to eat," said the pastor. "It's his nature."

"Can we at least keep the baby?" asked Fritz.

"Yes! We cannot leave it here to die; after all, we are to blame for its bad luck," said the pastor. "You take care of it, Fritz, and you will be responsible for it."

Fritz was happy to do so and decided to call his little monkey Knips.

CHAPTER 5

A FTER FAILING TO FIND THE MISSING CREW, THE FAMILY turned its attention to saving the animals on the ship. They built a small raft and they called it Deliverance. It was just large enough to fit the pastor, Fritz and hungry Knips, who had had nothing to eat since losing its mother. "Don't worry Knips," whispered Fritz. "We'll get you some milk!"

As soon as they got on the ship, Fritz kept his promise to the thirsty little monkey. The pastor looked on smiling as it drank from the goat.

"Well, that takes care of Knips," he said. "But what about the other animals? How can we take them to the island?"

"Wouldn't it be wonderful if they could all just swim across?" wondered Fritz.

They thought about it for a while, and then came up with an idea. Two casks were placed on each side of each animal. "What fine life jackets!" said the pastor before dropping the animals into the sea one by one. The creatures floated up and down in the water.

"I never thought I'd ever see something like this," said Fritz.

"I bet the animals did not expect it, either," said the pastor and began to paddle as Fritz pulled the floating animals with a rope. The cow, the donkey, the goats, the sheep, all seemed to be enjoying the cool sea water and followed obediently.

All of a sudden, the boy pointed to the sea. "We are lost!" he screamed. "A shark!"

The shark's fin could be seen circling the water, cutting through the waves like a sharp knife. It was quickly approaching the sheep. "Don't panic, Fritz," the pastor said. "Let's both shoot when it is close enough."

Fritz lifted his gun and waited. At his father's signal, they both aimed and fired. "Good!" cheered his father. The sea was painted red with the blood of the creature and then the wounded shark swam away, leaving a red trail behind .

"Do you think it will come back, Father?" asked Fritz. The pastor shrugged, but, to be on the safe side, they returned to the beach without wasting time. They relaxed only when they finally stepped on land and were reunited with Elizabeth and the rest of the family.

There were hugs and cheers, and plenty of amusement as the cow, donkey, goats and six sheep walked out of the sea, as though this was the most natural thing in the world. The younger boys laughed wildly at the sight, while the animals also looked happy now that they were finally on land.

Once the happy reunion was over, Jack shared a surprise. "Look what I made!" he said proudly, pointing to the belt he had created using animal skin.

"It looks great! How did you make it?" asked Fritz.

"Mother had packed a needle and thread in her magic bag," answered Jack.

There were more surprises at dinner; the main course was turtle eggs! "I found them on the beach. They are just like the ones Robinson Crusoe found on his island," said Ernest. "There are hundreds of them. And they taste delicious!"

Then, Elizabeth told her husband that, deeper in the forest, she had found a spot with beautiful tall trees. "Let's go there and make a tree house," she said. "Wouldn't it be fine to live so high up?"

"We are not birds, my dear," laughed the pastor. "How will we get up?"

"Do you remember a house that was built in a large tree near our house in Switzerland?" asked Elizabeth. "Do you remember how beautiful it was? Can you make stairs like the ones it had? It would be nice to sleep without worrying about jackals or any other dangerous animal."

The pastor could not refuse his wife so the next morning he set to work. He made a ladder using wood and ropes so that it could be pulled up at night. The boys also helped to make a bridge from the tent house to the tree house. The whole family worked hard for many days, but in the end they managed to build a large and comfortable house in the tree. When it was finished, they congratulated each other.

"Hurray, hurray, for our wonderful nest!" exclaimed Jack. "What a great house we will have up here!"

25

CHAPTER 6

EVERY DAY BROUGHT NEW DISCOVERIES AND THE FAMILY FELT more comfortable in their new home. "Let's give names to different areas. What do you think?" suggested the pastor one day. "The island may already have a name, so we'd better not name it. But we could name parts of it."

The boys found the idea brilliant. "Let's begin with the place where we first arrived," said Franz.

"We should call it Oyster Bay! Do you remember the oysters we found there? Do you remember how we used them as spoons?"

"No, let's call it Lobster Bay! Who can forget the giant lobster I caught and brought home?" asked Jack.

"No, let's call it Bay of Tears. Who can forget your tears when the lobster bit you?" laughed Ernest.

"Bay of Safety or Providence Bay would be more appropriate," said Elizabeth. "Remember that the place provided us with protection from the storm; and later we found many useful tools from the shipwreck there."

They went on and on like that for a long time, and gave names to almost every part of the island. They decided to call the tree house Falcon's Nest and the bridge they all helped to build was named Family Bridge. There were also other interesting names, such as Flamingo Marsh or Shark Island, and even Monkey Grove, where they had found little Knips.

Most days passed peacefully, but, as in all cases, there were some unfortunate events.

One day the pastor went to the far end of the island to take care of his crops. It was late when he returned to the tree house, almost past noon; when he got back, he noticed that it was awfully quiet, which was rather unusual.

Alarmed, he climbed the stairs and found the boys around their mother's bed, looking worriedly at her. Her eyes were closed, her face was pale and had an expression of pain.

"What happened?" asked the pastor anxiously, rushing to his wife's side.

All the boys started speaking at once and their father could understand nothing at all.

"Stop," he said. "Fritz, please explain."

"Mother was climbing down the stairs of Falcon's Nest, but she felt dizzy and she fell down and injured her right leg and her left foot," said the boy in one breath.

"She was in great pain," continued Ernest. "Fritz and I carried her to her bed right away, but the pain got worse."

"We didn't know what to do," added Jack. "I rubbed her foot, but it kept swelling."

"It hurts so much!" complained Elizabeth with a groan.

"Father, do you remember the medicine box from the ship? It must be in the tent house," said Ernest. "Maybe there's something there for Mother."

The pastor and Fritz immediately left for the tent house. When they returned a couple of hours later, Elizabeth's condition was worse. Her cheeks were very red, her eyes very bright and she had a fever.

To make matters worse, a storm had started and loud thunder was heard nearby.

The pastor opened the box to treat his wife's leg and foot. He put some cream on the sprained leg and tied it tightly with some pieces of cloth.

Elizabeth was in such pain that she fainted. At this, the pastor got very upset, but he tried to keep calm for the children's sake.

At that point, Franz came running to his mother's bed and hugged her.

"Wake up, Mama," he said. "We are all here – Papa and my brothers. There's a big storm and it frightens me. Open your eyes, Mama, please!"

His sweet voice helped Elizabeth wake up and, as soon as the storm passed, she was already feeling better.

Everybody felt relieved and promised to help around the house as much as they could.

In about two weeks' time, Elizabeth had completely recovered.

CHAPTER 7

LIFE ON THE ISLAND WAS HAPPY, BUT THE FAMILY NEVER GAVE up hope of meeting other people. They were always on the lookout for native people and passing ships.

"They're here! Savages at Providence Bay!" cried Jack one day. The pastor grabbed his gun and rushed to the tent house, ready for battle. A number of little figures were standing in a row along the water's edge. They appeared to be wearing dark coats and white waistcoats and stood quite still with their arms by their sides.

"Oh, Father!" exclaimed Jack excitedly. "I hope they are Lilliputians! I once read a book about these tiny people! Or are they pygmy natives?"

The pastor laughed at Jack's imagination. "I'm sorry to disappoint you, but they are penguins, dear Jack," he said, as they approached the creatures to have a better look. "They are excellent swimmers but cannot fly, or run when they are on land."

When father and son got closer, Jack started chasing the birds. He caught half a dozen, tied their legs and took them home to show the rest of the family. He was very proud of his catch, even though the pastor explained that penguin meat is not tasty because it has a strong fishy taste.

"Mother can make anything taste delicious!" insisted the boy all the way home.

However, they discovered sad news once they got back to Falcon's Nest. "Old Grizzle has disappeared," said Elizabeth sadly. "We cannot find our donkey anywhere. How will we manage to transport things without him?"

They all shook their heads in disappointment. They remembered how Grizzle had helped them build the bridge and transport heavy loads from one area to another. "How will we farm the land without old Grizzle?" cried Fritz.

Jack and his father immediately decided to look for the donkey. They followed its footprints but further away, they were mixed with other animal tracks. "What now?" asked Jack, looking at his father helplessly.

Before the pastor could answer, Turk and Ponto started barking excitedly at some animals in the distance. The pastor looked carefully and opened his mouth in amazement. "A herd of buffaloes!" he exclaimed.

Jack and his father carefully approached them and, with trembling hands, they shot at them. A huge roar was heard as the animals started running away. When the dust cloud disappeared, a wounded female buffalo was left lying on the ground with her young calf beside her.

Without wasting any time, Jack threw a lasso towards the calf and managed to catch its front legs. "If we tame it, we can use it instead of the donkey," he said to his father.

"First, we need to think of a way to take him back home," said the pastor. "Do you intend to carry him on your back?"

"I'm not Hercules!" joked the boy.

With its legs tied together the buffalo couldn't walk. The dogs held onto the animal's ears, keeping the head still so that the pastor managed to tie a rope around its neck and fasten it onto a tree. The buffalo fought for a long time, pulling at the rope and sometimes even banging his head on the tree. "Poor animal!" said Jack. "Do we really need to do this?" he asked his father.

"Yes," answered the man. "Don't worry, Jack," he added. "In a few hours, the young buffalo will be tame."

Indeed with time, the buffalo began to accept the situation. A few hours later, the animal had calmed down and when the pastor tried pulling it with the rope, it followed quietly.

At home, Elizabeth jumped in alarm when she saw the huge creature arrive with her husband and son. Fritz, Ernest and Franz watched with their mouths open. "Is it tame?" they asked.

"Not quite yet," said the pastor. "Not completely."

Before long, however, the buffalo was doing a number of jobs for the family. Even so, they never forgot their beloved Grizzle. "He was a good friend," said Franz. "I just hope he's alright."

The disappearance was a mystery, but the day they would find out what happened to their donkey was near.

CHAPTER 8

THE WEATHER WAS GETTING COOLER AND THE FAMILY BEGAN to wonder what winter would be like. They started preparing for the cold months ahead by collecting food. "We should find a warmer place to live in," suggested Elizabeth.

"But how will Grizzle find us if he comes back?" asked Franz, who had not given up hope of seeing his friend the donkey again.

Suddenly, they heard a strange noise near the tree house. "What's that?" whispered Franz. "Do you think there are savages out there?"

"Maybe it's just jackals," hoped Fritz.

"That is not the sound of jackals," said Ernest.

The pastor gathered the boys together as the noise continued. They all moved nearer to the spot from where the noises were heard, carefully hiding themselves. Fritz listened carefully with his gun ready and then, suddenly, he threw down his gun and roared with laughter. "Hey everyone," he called. "It's just old Grizzle!"

They all felt relieved and ran to Grizzle, welcoming him back with cheers and hugs. The donkey greedily ate the oats the boys gave him and gave out a loud "Hee-haw!"

"What's the matter, Grizzle? Did you get hungry?" asked Jack and they all laughed.

"Look, he has brought a friend, too," pointed the pastor. They all noticed Grizzle's companion shyly watching them. "Grizzle's friend is an onager, a wild donkey," said the pastor. "And, judging by the looks of this onager, I think old Grizzle is going to be a father!"

This news sent the boys cheering for joy and congratulating old Grizzle on his new family.

"Lucky Grizzle," whispered Ernest in the donkey's ear as he patted him on the back.

The pastor heard Ernest and said, "The only sure thing about luck is that it can easily change."

His words soon came true. It was not long before the donkey's luck changed for the worse.

Franz was the first to notice something long sliding on the sand towards the tree house. "There's something strange moving towards the bridge," said Franz. "It's quite big and long and it makes a hissing sound."

"Well, son, it sounds like a snake!" said the pastor, worried. "Where is it?"

The pastor grabbed his looking glass and examined the huge snake. "It is a boa constrictor. First, it grabs its prey and then wraps its body around it and strangles it before swallowing it whole," said the pastor, watching the snake move closer.

"How can we kill it?" asked Fritz.

"It is not so easy," said the pastor. "Let's just watch it for the moment."

The snake slowly moved towards the family. The boys and pastor all pointed at the snake with their guns until one of the boys fired, unable to resist. The other boys started shooting too. The snake moved quickly and disappeared into the bushes.

"It's gone!" shouted Franz.

"For now," said the pastor.

For three days and three nights the family stayed close together and the animals were tied up for their safety. Nobody was allowed to wander off alone and they decided to do only the most necessary jobs.

"Can I go out?" asked Jack one day. "There's no sign of the snake; it's gone."

"Don't be fooled," said the pastor. "The chickens and ducks are restless. This means that they still think it is around here somewhere."

Finally, they decided to cross the bridge together in order to get some animal feed from the tent house. When they untied Grizzle, he was so happy finally to be free that he ran around and around, and then into the trees. The family started calling him back but the donkey wouldn't listen.

Suddenly, the snake appeared and wrapped itself around his legs, quickly folding around him despite his brays and kicks.

"Shoot it, Father! Shoot it!" yelled the boys. "Save poor Grizzle!"

"It is too late!" said the pastor. "Our only hope is to kill him after he swallows Grizzle."

"How can a snake swallow a donkey?" asked Jack.

"Snakes cannot chew their food," explained the pastor. "They swallow them whole. In a little while, the snake will be too heavy to move. That's the best time for us to kill it."

It took a long time for the snake to finish its meal. When it finally ended, it lay on the ground, unable to move.

The family watched in horror. Then, Fritz, Ernest, Jack and the pastor waited and fired together. The snake rolled from side to side and then it stopped moving.

The boys cut it open and took out Grizzle's body. "Poor, Grizzle," said Ernest. "Your luck changed after all."

Upset because they had lost their beloved friend, they buried Grizzle on the spot and Jack made a sign to put on the donkey's grave. It read:

"Poor old Grizzle's final home
  He saved six lives
  By giving his own."

CHAPTER 9

WINTER CAME SOONER THAN THE FAMILY EXPECTED. WINDS shook the entire tree house and the rain fell through the roof. Wet, cold and scared, they were trying to find a solution.

"It might be better to move to the foot of the tree where we keep the food and gunpowder," suggested Elizabeth. They huddled into the small space, waiting for the rain to stop.

"Will it ever stop raining, Daddy?" asked Franz after days and days of heavy rain.

"Of course it will," said the pastor. To calm down and to pass the time, the family read one of the few books that they had saved from the shipwreck, the story of Robinson Crusoe. They had learnt a lot from the story. As they read it again, they decided to take Crusoe's example and find a cave as soon as the rain stopped.

"Yes, but when will the rain stop?" Franz kept asking until, quite unexpectedly, the sun came out of the clouds.

They were so happy to see sunshine after so many rainy weeks. The pastor, however, was worried. He knew that the worst was not over.

"We need to find a safe home fast," he said. "We shouldn't waste time. Winter has just started. Who knows when the rain will start again? We're in the tropics, do not forget that."

Jack and Fritz followed their father's orders and gathered hammers and axes. "We need to dig out a cave on higher ground," the pastor explained as they followed him up a hill. "It should be large enough for us and the animals."

It did not take them long to find the perfect spot. "Here!" said the pastor. The place had a beautiful view of Providence Bay and Family Bridge. "We will be able to see any passing ships from here," he said as he marked the wall of the rock.

Digging the rock was much harder work than they had expected. Five days passed, but they didn't make much progress.

However, after a few more days, the rock became easier to work with. "Am I getting better at digging or is this rock getting softer?" wondered Fritz.

A little later, Jack suddenly yelled: "I've made a hole in the wall!" He put his finger in it and tried to look through but he saw nothing. Then, they all started knocking at the side of the rock with their hammers and axes. Finally, a large hole was made, big enough for them to fit through.

"What are we waiting for? Let's go in, Father!" cried Jack.

"Not yet. It might be dangerous," said the pastor.

"Why? Do you suppose there are lions or bears inside?" asked Fritz. "We have our guns; we'll be fine."

"Don't be silly!" exclaimed the pastor. "It's not wild animals. It's the air I'm afraid of. It may be poisonous."

"Let's make the hole larger, so that the bad air leaves," said Fritz.

"The best way to clean the air is to light a fire in the cave. When the bad air leaves, the fire will burn freely," said the pastor.

The boys threw dry grass in the cave and then lit a match. A loud explosion followed and then a few smaller ones.

When the explosions stopped and they knew it was safe, they entered the cave. The sides of the cave sparkled at the light from their torches. "Diamonds!" exclaimed Jack enthusiastically.

"Crystals," explained the pastor. The sight was amazing. In some places the light through the crystals shone with all the colours of the rainbow. The cave looked magical. It had three large spaces, one leading to another, which they could use as rooms.

The boys jumped up and down with joy. "Yes! We can stop digging!" they cheered.

Then Elizabeth, Ernest and Franz came to see their new home. Outside the cave the mother admired the view, but the real surprise was inside.

Elizabeth was not prepared for the beauty she saw. There were crystals glittering all around her and the stalactites on the roof looked like small statues.

In the middle of the large room was a big stone like a table, large enough for the entire family to sit at and eat together.

Elizabeth closed her eyes and took a deep breath. "Oh, my!" she exclaimed, hearing her voice echo back to her.

"My wishes have come true," she said with tears in her eyes. "I never imagined a home as beautiful as this." She looked at her family and felt very happy. "We are the richest people in the world!" she smiled.

CHAPTER 10

CAPTAIN JOHNSON AND LIEUTENANT BELL STAYED UP LATE reading the pastor's journal. "It all sounds too good to be true," said Captain Johnson. "This island seems like a paradise on earth. They eat like kings, have learnt to make all sorts of things like candles and clothes. The only thing they haven't made is chocolate!"

"Yes, but they are so isolated and alone," said Lieutenant Bell. "The pastor was very interested to learn about what was going on in the rest of the world. It must be very hard to be away from your country for so long."

"They've done a good job making this island their new country," said Captain Johnson. "I can only imagine what their beautiful cave is like. My travels have taken me to many interesting places, but I have never heard of a crystal cave which is used as a home. I'd like to see all the family's homes, as well as their crops."

Unfortunately, this never happened. The two seamen went to sleep and soon after a new storm began. Waves beat the ship, tossing it here and there. Once again, they thought that they would be lost forever as they rushed around trying to save themselves and the ship. At one point, the anchor was cut and their ship was blown far away. When the storm was over, the island was nowhere to be seen.

"Do you think we can get back to the Swiss Family of Robinson Crusoes?" Lieutenant Bell asked Captain Johnson once they were safe.

"We have no idea where they are," said Captain Johnson. "From what we know, the seas around the island are very dangerous. It would be foolish to go back. Even if we did, we might not be able to find them."

"Oh, I wonder... what do you think will become of them?" said Lieutenant Bell.

Captain Johnson smiled. "Don't worry about them, Lieutenant Bell," he said. "They are just fine in their beautiful cave palace. I wish I had such a home too!"

"We must find the pastor's brother in Switzerland," said Lieutenant

Bell. "We must give him the diary so that he knows that they're still alive."

"It is the least we can do. If I were lost on some island, I, too, would like someone to tell my dear wife that I am alive and well," said the captain.

The two seamen stared at the calm sea in silence. They were both thinking about the surprises and adventures they would have to face before finally returning home to their loved ones.

"This voyage is taking longer than I had expected," said Captain Johnson, suddenly feeling homesick.

"Indeed, it is," answered Lieutenant Bell as he watched the sun set in the deep waters of the Pacific.

CHAPTER 1

Comprehension

1 **Decide if the following statements are True or False. Write T or F in the boxes.**

1. Lieutenant Bell's wife was pleased that her husband was a sailor. ☐

2. When the Adventurer reached the island, the crew thought they were the first men on it. ☐

3. The pastor was thrilled that someone had finally found him and his family. ☐

4. The Swiss family went to the island in order to start a new life. ☐

5. The pastor's wife and children didn't know that a ship had found them. ☐

2 **Choose a, b or c to complete the following sentences.**

1. Lieutenant Bell
   a. had no children.
   b. didn't like being a sailor.
   c. had faced a lot of difficulties during his voyages.

2. The Swiss pastor
   a. looked unfriendly at first.
   b. has been on the island for more than two years.
   c. didn't want to leave the island.

3. Lieutenant Bell and his men
   a. were on their way to England when a storm stopped them.
   b. didn't find anyone on the island.
   c. decided not to help the Swiss family.

4. The pastor
   a. had three children.
   b. had no brothers or sisters.
   c. had a brother back in his country.

5. Bell's ship
   a. was travelling in the Mediterranean Sea when the storm started.
   b. went to the island to escape the storm.
   c. couldn't anchor near the island.

Vocabulary

3 **Complete the sentences using the words in the box.**

swallow beg struggle blow crash discuss rush

1. John _____ his car last night. Luckily, he wasn't injured at all.

2. It is raining heavily and the wind _____ hard. Let's go back home before it gets any worse!

3. You should always _____ your problems with your family and friends. They will help you.

4. The little boy didn't want to _____ the medicine. It was awful!

5. The children _____ down the stairs in order to welcome their mother.

6. The fish _____ to get back into the water.

7. My sister _____ me not to tell our parents that she had broken the window.

4 **Find the words in Chapter 1 to match the definitions below. The first letter has been given to you.**

1. All the people working on a ship or plane   c _____ (page 4)

2. Something that can be seen   v _____ (page 4)

3. Material used for making shoes, bags etc. l _____ (page 6)

4. The act of leaving a place   d _____ (page 6)

5. Be very pleased or excited about something t _____ (page 6)

Follow-up activities

5 **Discuss.**

1. Why did Bell's wife beg him not to go on another voyage? How would you feel if you were in her position?

2. What happened during Bell's last trip? Would you ever choose to be a sailor? Why/Why not?

3. How did the pastor feel when he saw the ship? How would you feel if you were shipwrecked on an island for so long?

4. Why didn't the pastor tell his family about the ship? Would you do the same? Why/Why not?

6 **Imagine that you are Lieutenant Bell, returning to the Adventurer after meeting the pastor. Write an entry in your diary, describing the man and the feelings the meeting with him caused you. (60-80 words)**

CHAPTER 2

Comprehension

1 **Answer the following questions.**

1. What happened to the pastor's ship?

   _____

2. What happened when the family went up on deck to board the lifeboats?

   _____

3. What did the family find after searching through the ship?

   _____

4. What was Jack's idea for getting to the island and what did the rest of the family think about it?

   _____

5. What did the pastor decide to do with the animals?

   _____

2 **Match 1-5 with a-e to make sentences. Write a-e in the boxes.**

1. The pastor advised ☐
2. When they woke up ☐
3. They decided ☐
4. Suddenly, Jack ☐
5. As they were about to leave, ☐

a. was heard screaming!

b. to search the ship for equipment.

c. the pastor's wife dropped a mysterious bag in the barrel.

d. his wife and children to be calm.

e. they saw some land nearby.

Vocabulary

3 **Fill in the blanks with the correct form of the words in capital.**

1. _____, there were no survivors from the plane crash.   **FORTUNATE**

2. Suddenly, the magician made the two birds _____.   **APPEAR**

3. I am so _____ for your generous gift.   **THANK**

4. We were all very _____ to hear that Gary was safe.   **RELIEF**

5. Are you sure you have all the _____ to go rock climbing?   **EQUIP**

6. Martin's advice was really _____.   **USE**
I don't know what I'd do without him.

4 Choose a, b or c to complete the sentences below.

1. Oh look! My shoes are _____ to yours!
   a. monstrous   **b.** mysterious   **c.** similar

2. The man _____ my hand and said to me, "I am so happy to meet you!"
   a. tossed   **b.** shook   **c.** announced

3. There were not enough _____ for all the passengers on the ship.
   a. lifeboats   **b.** crew   **c.** decks

4. "Please don't _____ at me, I'm not shouting at you," said the boy.
   a. rush   **b.** leap   **c.** yell

5. The man hit the nail with a _____ and forced it into the wood.
   a. hammer   **b.** raft   **c.** hook

6. I stayed _____ all night long thinking about the exams.
   a. unexpected   **b.** exhausted   **c.** awake

7. Teri _____ that something bad had happened and she called her sister to see if she was alright.
   a. fought   **b.** feared   **c.** floated

Follow-up activities

5 Discuss.

1. How did the family feel when they realised they were all alone on the ship? How would you have reacted in a situation like that?

2. What do you think of Jack's idea for reaching the island? What other ways would you have suggested?

3. What equipment or things would you consider useful for living on a remote island?

4. What do you think that the family will do once they get to the island?

6 Imagine that you are Fritz. You want to send a letter in a bottle in the hope that someone will find it and come to your rescue. Write a letter saying what has happened to you and asking for help. (60-80 words)

CHAPTER 3

Comprehension

1 **Complete the sentences with the correct name.**

Elizabeth	Jack	Fritz	The pastor	Ernest

1. _____ found a lobster while he was looking for shellfish.
2. _____ came back from hunting carrying an agouti.
3. _____ prepared some soup for the family.
4. _____ found some oysters and he also found salt.
5. _____ showed Jack how to make oysters open.
6. _____ screamed at the dogs and kicked them for killing the agouti.
7. _____ separated the salt from the dirt.

2 **Put the following events in the order which they happened. Write 1-6 in the boxes.**

a. Jack ate his first oyster but he didn't like it at all. ☐

b. Ernest set off to look for more "spoons" for their meal. ☐

c. Elizabeth started making dinner. ☐

d. The dogs killed the agouti. ☐

e. The family made their home near the river. ☐

f. Jack killed a lobster with a stone. ☐

Vocabulary

3 **Complete the sentences using the prepositions in the box.**

under	with	for	by	from	through	about	to

1. Last night, my friends and I had a delicious three-course meal _____ dinner.
2. Today, Jim learned some really interesting things _____ dolphins at school.
3. Andrew was able to open the door _____ using the key that Sam gave him.

4. There are some animals that live _____ the ground.

5. I mixed the powder _____ some water and made a very tasty soup!

6. Tim's house is very close _____ the railway station.

7. The thief got into the house _____ the kitchen window.

8. Henry's son ran and hugged his father when he returned _____ his long journey.

4 **Find the words in Chapter 3 which mean the same as:**

1. near, easy to reach, not causing
   difficulty   _____ (page 12)

2. gate or door by which people
   enter a place   _____ (page 12)

3. Very tasty   _____ (page 12)

4. The hard nut-like fruit of a tropical
   tree   _____ (page 14)

5. a strong feeling which shows that
   you aren't pleased about sth   _____ (page 14)

6. disagreed, objected, argued   _____ (page 15)

Follow-up activities

5 **Discuss.**

1. What do you think of hunting ? Are you for or against animal hunting?

2. How do you feel about Fritz's behaviour towards the dogs after they killed the agouti? Was he right to react like that?

3. Do you agree with the pastor's comment that nature is unfair? What you think that he meant?

4. What do you think that the family will do in the next chapter?

6 **Imagine you are Jack. Write an entry in your diary about all the things you did on your first day on the island. (60-80 words)**

CHAPTER 4

Comprehension

1 **Read Chapter 4 and match the two halves of the sentences. Write a-e in the boxes.**

1. The pastor decided ☐
2. Fritz suggested ☐
3. The monkeys started ☐
4. The pastor and his son discovered ☐
5. Fritz agreed ☐

a. throwing coconuts at the pastor and his son.
b. to take care and be responsible for the baby monkey
c. saving the animals on the ship first.
d. to spend the day looking for the rest of the people on the ship.
e. some gourds with which they could make plates and kitchen utensils.

2 **Complete the summary of Chapter 4 using the words in the box.**

| sugar cane   snarls   gourd   flamingos   explore   crew |
| coconuts   frightened   utensils |

Fritz and the pastor set off to (**1**) _____ the area and look for the missing (**2**) _____. They took their guns and Turk with them for protection. While they were walking, Fritz was excited to see there were (**3**) _____ up on the trees. Some monkeys that were also on the trees helped them get the fruit. They threw rocks at the animals and they, in return, started throwing coconuts at them. Later on, the pastor and his son found (**4**) _____ which made the coconut milk taste delicious. After a while, they found a very useful fruit called (**5**) _____ with which they could make plates and kitchen (**6**) _____. They also saw some (**7**) _____ which didn't seem (**8**) _____ at all. This made the pastor realise that no people had ever visited the island. Suddenly, they heard Turk's (**9**) _____ and saw Turk killing the mother of a baby monkey. They decided to keep the little monkey and call it Knips.

Vocabulary

3 **Choose a, b or c to complete the sentences below.**

1. "What a beautiful dress!" Mary _____ as soon as she saw me.
   a. threw   b. exclaimed   c. laughed

50

2. Her mother _____ the little girl for lying to her.
   a. punished   **b.** begged   **c.** hugged

3. Stop treating Timothy so _____! He is not the one to blame for the accident!
   a. naturally   **b.** calmly   **c.** cruelly

4. " Don't eat that fruit. It's very _____!" Tammy said to her daughter.
   a. safe   **b.** sour   **c.** fresh

4 **Complete the crossword with words from Chapter 4.**

1. When sugar (in food, beer, wine etc.) changes into alcohol
2. To make an angry sound while showing your teeth
3. A person, esp. a child or animal, whose parents have died
4. The thick wooden part of a tree
5. Very hot weather, high temperature
6. A liquid made from sour wine which we use in cooking
7. The opposite of "wet"
8. To damage, ruin completely

Follow-up activities

5 **Discuss.**

1. The pastor knows many things that help the family survive on the island. Do you know any useful tips that would help if you were shipwrecked on an island?

2. The pastor made plates with a gourd shell and sand. Can you make anything out of simple things? What arts and crafts can you do? Who taught you these things?

3. How do you feel about Turk killing a monkey? Would you have felt like Fritz did?

4. What do you think happened to the missing crew? Will the Swiss family find any of them in the next chapters?

6 **Imagine that you are Fritz. You want to write a letter to your friend, Ben, telling him about the exciting day you've just had, in the hope that soon you will be able to send it to him. (60-80 words)**

CHAPTER 5

Comprehension

1 Complete the summary of Chapter 5 with the sentences a-e.

a. Then, Jack showed Fritz and his father the leather belt he had made.

b. They got to the island and all the family were very happy that they had managed to save all the animals.

c. They decided to make a tree house.

d. There was a shark circling the water.

e. The pastor took Fritz and the hungry monkey along with him and they all got to the ship on the raft.

After having searched for the missing crew with no success, the family decided to save the animals on the ship. For that reason, they built a raft which they called Deliverance. (1) _____. There, little Knips was able to drink milk from a goat. Then, they used casks as life jackets so that the animals could float. Suddenly, Fritz pointed to the sea very frightened. (2) _____. Luckily, they fired and injured it and the wounded shark swam away. They were safe. (3) _____. They hugged them and cheered and laughed a lot. (4) _____. Ernest shared another surprise; he had found delicious turtle eggs on the beach which they would have for dinner! Elizabeth also told her husband about the tall trees that she had seen deeper in the forest. (5) _____. There, they could sleep without worrying about dangerous animals.

2 Answer the following questions.

1. How did the pastor and his son manage to bring the animals to the island?

2. What did Fritz and the pastor do when they saw the shark?

3. What surprises did Jack and Ernest have for Fritz and their father when they got back to the island?

4. What did Elizabeth suggest that they should make and why?

5. What else did the family make working together?

Vocabulary

3 **Choose the correct word to complete the following sentences.**

1. Kate and Courtney were **whispering / wondering** in the corner so that nobody could hear them.

2. Yesterday, Henry and I used my father's canoe and **floated / paddled** as far as the opposite island.

3. Gina's dog always follows her orders **obediently / wildly**.

4. While Tracy was sewing a button, she hurt her finger with the **thread / needle**.

5. Larry managed to get to the roof of the house using a long, wooden **bridge / ladder**.

6. The little boy just **refused / shrugged** when his father asked him where Helen was.

4 **Find the opposites of the words below in Chapter 5.**

1. awful, horrible _____ (page 21)

2. far away _____ (page 22)

3. calm _____ (page 22)

4. dangerous _____ (page 22)

5. ugly _____ (page 24)

6. accept _____ (page 24)

Follow-up activities

5 **Discuss.**

1. Fritz said that he never thought he would ever see animals floating up and down in the water. What is the strangest thing you have seen in your life?

2. What would you do if you were in the middle of the sea and saw a shark? What do you know about sharks?

3. What do you think of Elizabeth's idea to build a tree house? Would you like to have a tree house? Why/Why not?

4. Do you think the family will be safe in the tree house? What are the problems they might face there?

6 **Imagine that you are Ernest. Write a diary entry describing the tree house and the advantages and disadvantages of your new home. (60-80 words)**

53

CHAPTER 6

Comprehension

1 Choose a, b or c to complete the following sentences.

1. The family decided
   a. to explore new areas.
   b. to give a name to the island.
   c. to name the different areas on the island.

2. Elizabeth was climbing down the stairs of the tree house when
   a. she fell down and injured her head.
   b. she injured her foot and her leg.
   c. a loud thunder frightened her and she fell down.

3. Elizabeth's sons
   a. got very upset when she fainted
   b. treated their mother's leg and foot
   c. were all very afraid of the storm

4. Fritz
   a. suggested looking for medicine in the tent house.
   b. carried his mother to her bed with the help of Ernest.
   c. hugged his mother when she fainted.

5. As soon as the storm passed,
   a. Elizabeth recovered completely.
   b. Elizabeth woke up.
   c. Elizabeth was feeling better.

2 Match 1-5 with a-e to make true sentences.
   Write a-e in the boxes.

1. One day, the pastor went to the far end of the island ☐
2. The pastor got back to the tree house and ☐
3. The boys were around their mother's bed ☐
4. Jack rubbed his mother's foot but ☐
5. Elizabeth fainted because ☐

   a. it kept swelling.
   b. looking worriedly at her.
   c. she was in a lot of pain.
   d. everything was awfully quiet.
   e. to take care of his crops.

54

Vocabulary

3 **Fill in the blanks with the correct form of the words in capital.**

1. The three climbers found a place of _____ to spend the stormy night. **SAFE**

2. You must always wear a helmet when you ride a motorbike for _____. **PROTECT**

3. Those poor _____ people have nowhere to live. They have to sleep in the street! **FORTUNE**

4. "Oh no! What has happened to your car?" Jim asked Kelly looking _____ at her. **WORRY**

5. When Ben saw his mother's _____, he immediately knew that he was in trouble. **EXPRESS**

4 **Find the words in Chapter 6 that mean the same as:**

1. correct or suitable _____ (page 26)

2. face or skin having a rather white colour _____ (page 26)

3. rare, not common or ordinary _____ (page 26)

4. have a feeling that things go round and round _____ (page 28)

5. no longer worried _____ (page 28)

6. closely, firmly _____ (page 28)

Follow-up activities

5 **Discuss.**

1. Would you like to give names to a place or an animal? What name would you choose if you had a pet? How would you name your favourite place?

2. What would you do to help Elizabeth after the accident? Do you know anything about First Aid?

3. Have you ever had an accident? If so, what happened to you and how did you feel? Did you recover quickly?

4. How do you think the boys felt after their mother's accident? How would you feel in their place?

6 **Imagine you are Elizabeth. Write a diary entry describing your accident and how you felt. (60-80 words)**

CHAPTER 7

Comprehension

1 Decide if the following statements are True or False. Write T or F in the boxes.

1. The Swiss family were so happy on the island that they didn't care about finding other people. ☐

2. One day, Jack and the pastor saw some penguins near the tree house. ☐

3. From far, the penguins looked like people. ☐

4. The pastor said that penguins are delicious because they taste like fish. ☐

5. The family were very disappointed because they lost their donkey, Grizzle. ☐

6. The pastor wanted to tame a buffalo and use it instead of the donkey. ☐

7. The family forgot about the donkey as soon as they found the buffalo. ☐

2 Put the following events in the order which they happened. Write 1-5 in the boxes.

a. The pastor tied a rope around a calf's neck and fastened it onto a tree. ☐

b. The calf calmed down and the pastor pulled it home. ☐

c. Jack and his father met a herd of buffaloes and shot at them. ☐

d. Jack and the pastor caught some penguins and took them home to show the rest of the family. ☐

e. Elizabeth told Jack and her husband that Old Grizzle, the donkey, had disappeared. ☐

Vocabulary

3 Complete the sentences with the correct form of the words in the box.

grab appear approach chase transport tame

1. We _____ the house silently as we didn't want to be seen or heard by anyone.

56

2. People have always wanted to _____ wild animals.

3. The two thieves _____ the money and left the bank quickly.

4. We were worried that they wouldn't come but they finally _____ at the last minute.

5. It was so funny watching the cat _____ the dog. We couldn't stop laughing!

6. Martha's husband is a truck driver. He _____ wood from forests to the factory.

4 **Read the definitions below and find the words in Chapter 7.**

1. a fight between enemies _____ (page 30)

2. a line (of people or things) standing side by side _____ (page 30)

3. very small _____ (page 30)

4. footprints _____ (page 31)

5. a deep, loud continuing sound _____ (page 32)

Follow-up activities

5 **Discuss.**

1. At first, when Jack saw the penguins, he thought that they were pygmies or Lilliputians. Have you read *Gulliver's Travels* or seen a film under the same title? Have you ever heard stories about little people before?

2. Jack and his father met a herd of buffalos. Have you ever seen a wild animal? If so, where and when? If not, would you like to? What do you think you would do?

3. Have you ever eaten any kind of strange food like penguin meat? If so, what did you eat? What did it taste like? If not, would you like to taste something strange? What would that be?

4. What do you think that happened to Grizzle? Do you think that the Swiss family will find their beloved donkey?

6 **Imagine that you are Jack. Write an entry in your diary describing your experience with the young buffalo and the feelings the loss of Grizzle caused you. (60-80 words)**

CHAPTER 8

Comprehension

1 Read the sentences and find the words. Then write them in the spaces provided. The word in the red boxes is a wild donkey.

1. A person who spends time with another, a friend
2. Move about without having a particular destination
3. Fold round a body
4. Collect, bring people together
5. The act or sound of laughing
6. To cover with soil

2 Old Grizzle has just been buried after being eaten by a snake. Imagine you are Fritz. Complete his diary with a word or short phrase.

A few days ago, we were too relieved to have Old Grizzle back. He had a female companion with him. We realised that he was going to be (**1**) _____! Unfortunately, his luck soon changed for (**2**) _____. A long snake appeared near the tree house. We tried to kill it, but the snake disappeared (**3**) _____. We all stayed together for three days and we tied up the animals for (**4**) _____. When we (**5**) _____ Grizzle, he ran into the trees. The snake found him and (**6**) _____ itself around his legs. We couldn't do anything to (**7**) _____ the donkey, so we just watched in horror. When the snake finished its meal, we (**8**) _____ it dead. We took Grizzle's body, buried our beloved friend and put a sign on (**9**) _____. We were very upset that we lost him.

Vocabulary

3 Choose a, b or c to complete the sentences below.

1. They all _____ David on his promotion. He really deserved it.
   a. patted   **b.** judged   **c.** congratulated

2. Sam can never _____ chocolate ice-cream. He likes it so much!
   a. resist   **b.** cheer   **c.** strangle

3. "Stop eating so _____ ! It looks as if you haven't eaten in weeks!" Mary said to her son.
   a. shyly   **b.** easily   **c.** greedily

4. Last night, we watched a documentary about how lions catch their
_____.

   a. bray   **b.** prey   **c.** bush

5. John is a very _____ person. He is never relaxed, even when he is on holiday!

   a. necessary   **b.** restless   **c.** upset

4 **Complete the following sentences using the prepositions in the box.**

ahead of on back towards at into

1. The hunter pointed _____ the rabbit with his gun but it quickly disappeared _____ the forest.

2. Even though it was dark, we could clearly see three masked men running _____ the bank so we immediately called the police.

3. "Welcome _____, Mum! Dad and I have really missed you," said Joey to his mother when she arrived.

4. We could see a light shining _____, so we knew we were approaching the village.

5. When the boss announced that I had got the job, everyone came and patted me _____ the back.

6. Although six months had already passed, Donna never gave up hope _____ finding her missing dog.

Follow-up activities

5 **Discuss.**

1. Have you ever had a pet and lost it? If so, did it come back? If not, what do you think it's like to lose a pet?

2. The pastor said, "The only sure about luck is that it can easily change"? Do you agree with that comment? Have you ever experienced a sudden change of luck?

3. How do you think the family felt watching the boa eating the donkey? How would you react in a situation like that?

4. What do you think the pastor and his family will do to protect themselves from the cold winter in the next chapter?

6 **Imagine you are Ernest. Write a story about Grizzle and his unlucky death. (60-80 words)**

CHAPTER 9

Comprehension

1 Complete the summary of Chapter 9 with the sentences a-e.

a. the sun came out of the clouds
b. big enough for them to fit through
c. they were the richest people in the world
d. sooner than the Swiss family expected
e. so they lit a fire

Winter came (**1**) _____ and they were trying to find a solution to protect themselves from the cold and the rain. After many rainy weeks, (**2**) _____ and, without wasting any time, the family found a perfect spot to dig out a cave. Digging the rock was much harder work than they had thought but, after a few days, they managed to make a hole which was (**3**) _____. The pastor then knew that they had to clean the air in the cave, (**4**) _____. When they knew it was safe, they entered the cave which looked magical! When Elizabeth came to see their new house, she really believed that (**5**) _____.

2 Answer the following questions.

1. How did the family feel during the rainy days?

2. In what way did the family follow Robinson Crusoe's example?

3. What did the pastor suggest they should do for the winter?

4. In what way was the spot the family found perfect?

5. Why didn't the pastor let his sons go into the cave immediately after they opened the hole?

6. In what sense did the cave look magical?

Vocabulary

3 Choose a, b or c to complete the sentences below.

1. "Don't eat that berry, Joey! It may be _____!" shouted his mother.
   a. entire   **b.** poisonous   **c.** magical

2. A diamond ring _____ on Laura's finger.
   a. fitted   **b.** admired   **c.** glittered

3. The two little puppies _____ together to keep warm.
   a. huddled   **b.** echoed   **c.** sparkled

4. The children ran _____ in the streets as there weren't any cars.
   a. enthusiastically   **b.** unexpectedly   **c.** freely

5. I'm very happy with the _____ Betty is making. If she keeps up the good work, she'll surely pass the exams.
   a. progress   **b.** explosion   **c.** order

4 Choose the correct word to complete the following sentences.

1. My father used a(n) **hammer / axe** to cut down the huge tree in our garden.

2. Jonathan and I will visit Paris again this Christmas! It is our favourite holiday **spot / ground**.

3. The earthquake was so strong that our house was **shaking / wasting** for about 30 seconds!

4. Can you hear somebody **leading / knocking** on the door?

5. It is important for students to have a teacher they **mark / admire**.

Follow-up activities

5 Discuss.

1. During rainy days, the Swiss family read a book in order to calm down and pass their time. What is your favourite pastime activity? How do rainy days make you feel?

2. What do you think of the family's idea to dig out a cave to protect themselves from the bad weather? What other ways would you have suggested if you were in a situation like this?

3. The family were very excited when they saw their new "house". Have you ever explored a cave? What do you think that living in a cave would be like? Would you like it? Why/Why not?

4. What do you believe that will happen in the final Chapter?

6 Imagine you are Elizabeth. Write a diary entry describing what you saw when you entered the cave and how you felt. (60-80 words)

CHAPTER 10

Comprehension

1 **Decide if the following statements are True or False. Write T or F in the boxes.**

1. Captain Johnson and Lieutenant Bell believed that life on the island must be great. ☐

2. The Swiss family learned to make almost everything by themselves. ☐

3. Captain Johnson once saw a crystal cave which was used as a home. ☐

4. When the new storm began, Captain Johnson and Lieutenant Bell thought they would die. ☐

5. The two seamen agreed to find the pastor's brother in Switzerland. ☐

2 **Read the definitions below and find the words in Chapter 7.**

1. "Unfortunately, **this** never happened." (page 42)

   _____

2. "Even if we did, we might not be able to find **them**." (page 42)

   _____

3. "I wish I had **such a home** too!" (page 42) _____

4. "**It** is the least we can do" (page 43) _____

5. "Indeed, **it** is." (page 43) _____

Vocabulary

3 **Complete the following sentences using the prepositions in the box.**

away   of   about   at   around

1. Although Tim and I had never heard _____ that restaurant before, we decided to visit it. It was really great!

2. Gabriela's house is only one mile _____ from mine so I'll go and visit her on my bike!

3. "Why is that boy staring _____ you, Jessica? Do you know him?" Kate asked her.

4. Leonardo Da Vinci must have been a really interesting person. I want to learn everything _____ his life.

5. The Johnsons own a wonderful house in the countryside. It has got all kinds of trees _____ it!

4 **Find the words in Chapter 10 to match the definitions below. The first letter has been given for you.**

1. A daily record of events, a diary   j _____ (page 42)

2. Something that is burned to give us light   c _____ (page 42)

3. Away from other people or buildings   i _____ (page 42)

4. Something (e.g. fruit or vegetables) that a farmer grows   c _____ (page 42)

5. Kind of silly   f _____ (page 42)

6. Having a strong wish to be at home, when sb is away from it   h _____ (page 43)

Follow-up activities

5 **Discuss.**

1. What did Captain Johnson think when he finished reading the pastor's diary? Do you agree with him? Why?/Why not?

2. What happened after Captain Johnson and Lieutenant Bell went to sleep? What happened to the Adventurer?

3. What do the two seamen want to do as soon as they get back home? Would you do the same? Why/Why not?

4. How do you think the pastor and his family will react when they discover that the ship is gone? How would you react if you were in their position?

6 **Imagine you are Lieutenant Bell. Write a letter to the pastor's brother in Switzerland arranging for you to meet and give him the pastor's diary. Tell him about the pastor, his family and their life on the island (60-80 words)**

Swiss Family Robinson
Student's Book
by Johann David Wyss adapted by H.Q. Mitchell

Published by: **MM Publications**
                  www.mmpublications.com
                  info@mmpublications.com

Offices
UK Cyprus France Greece Poland Turkey USA
Associated companies and representatives throughout the world.

Produced in the EU

ISBN: 978-960-509-100-2   C1211006032-7013